Making Water Safe

Nellie Wilder

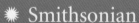
Smithsonian

Consultants

Brian Mandell
Program Specialist
Smithsonian Science Education Center

Chrissy Johnson, M.Ed.
Teacher, Cedar Point Elementary
Prince William County Schools, Virginia

Sara Cooper, M.Ed.
Third Grade Teacher
Fullerton School District

Publishing Credits

Rachelle Cracchiolo, M.S.Ed., *Publisher*
Conni Medina, M.A.Ed., *Editor in Chief*
Diana Kenney, M.A.Ed., NBCT, *Series Developer*
Emily R. Smith, M.A.Ed., *Content Director*
Véronique Bos, *Creative Director*
Robin Erickson, *Art Director*
Michelle Jovin, M.A., *Associate Editor*
Mindy Duits, *Series Designer*
Kevin Panter, *Senior Graphic Designer*
Smithsonian Science Education Center

Image Credits: back cover D. Zheleva/Shutterstock; p.8 diy13/ Shutterstock; p.10 Radius Images/Alamy; p.11 (bottom) Keith Homan/ Shutterstock; p.11 (middle) Prabhjit S. Kalsi/Shutterstock; p.12 Rikflikpix/ Alamy; p.13 Delimont Photography/Newscom; p.14 STRDEL/AFP/ Getty Images; p.16 Keystone Pictures USA ZUMA Press/Newscom; p.19 qaphotos.comAlamy; all other images from iStock and/or Shutterstock.

Library of Congress Cataloging-in-Publication Data

Names: Rice, Dona, author. | Smithsonian Institution.
Title: Making water safe / Dona Herweck Rice.
Description: Huntington Beach, CA : Teacher Created Materials, 2019. | Audience: K to grade 3. | Copyrighted 2020 by the Smithsonian Institution.
 | Identifiers: LCCN 2018049788 (print) | LCCN 2018050952 (ebook) | ISBN 9781493868964 (eBook) | ISBN 9781493866564 (pbk.)
Subjects: LCSH: Drinking water--Juvenile literature. | Water-supply--Juvenile
 literature. | Water--Juvenile literature.
Classification: LCC TD348 (ebook) | LCC TD348 .R53 2019 (print) | DDC 628.1/62--dc23
LC record available at https://lccn.loc.gov/2018049788

Table of Contents

Water Is Life

Some people say water is life. We all need water to live.

People need water to drink. They need it to grow and make food. People need water to keep clean too.

A boy drinks water from a glass.

These girls water plants.

A girl washes her hands to keep clean.

Science & Mathematics

Water Needs

People need at least 8 **liters** (2 gallons) of water each day. That is enough for drinking and cooking. But to stay clean, it takes more than twice that amount of water.

Not all people have clean water. That is a big problem in the world.

Dirty water flows out of these pipes.

DANGER

DO NOT
DRINK
THIS WATER

The water in this lake is dirty.

Clean Water

People want to fix this problem. They want clean water for all.

A scientist holds dirty water and clean water.

Scientists study clean water.

Learning from Plants

Plants can clean water. People have made straws that **filter** water like plants. The straws make water safer to drink.

Some fixes are simple. These women use their clothes. They fold **cloth** and pour water through it. The cloth acts like a filter.

This girl uses cloth as a filter.

This woman uses her khimar to filter water.

On Tap

Clean water is easy with **taps**. Pipes and filters bring clean water to you.

These pails are filters.
They are packed with layers
of earth. The layers filter
the water. Plants clean
water with their layers too.

This woman waits for
the pails to filter water.

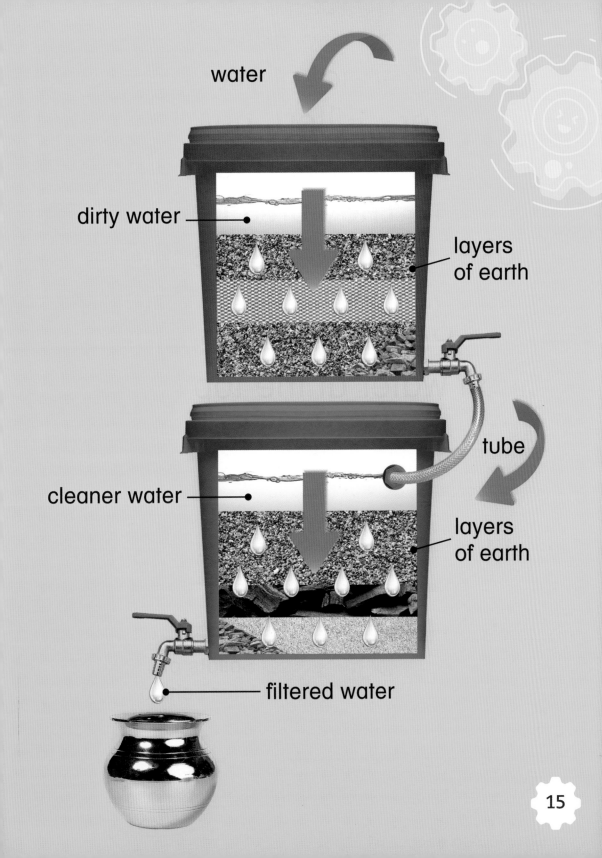

water

dirty water

layers of earth

cleaner water

tube

layers of earth

filtered water

15

People cannot drink saltwater. Filters help! People put saltwater in the bottom. The sun's heat makes clean water rise to the top. The salt does not rise. People can drink the clean water at the top.

Sailors pull a saltwater filter behind their boat.

Pour saltwater into the bottom of the filter.

The sun's heat causes water to rise to the top.

Pour out clean water.

Water for All

All of us should have clean water. People are hard at work to make sure we get it!

A girl drinks clean water from a tap.

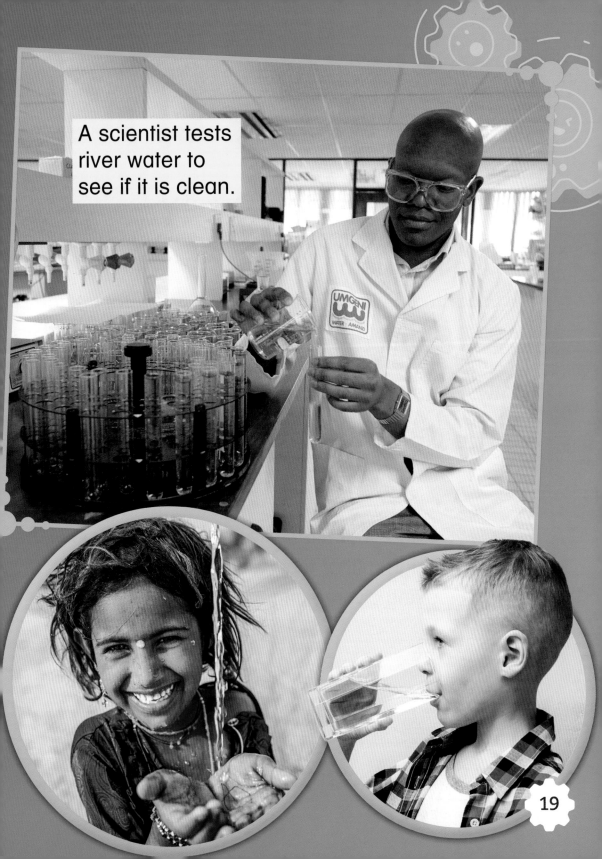

A scientist tests river water to see if it is clean.

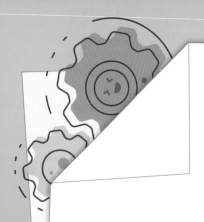

STEAM CHALLENGE

The Problem

Your team wants to bring clean water to a place that does not have it. But you need a simple way to filter the water! Make a filter that can clean water so that someone can drink it.

The Goals

- Design a filter that can separate water from rocks and dirt.
- Design your filter with any materials you want.
- Design a filter that will clean water without leaking or breaking.

Research and Brainstorm

What materials can filter water? What shape should a filter be so water will not spill?

Design and Build

Draw your plan. How will it work? What materials will you use? Build your filter!

Test and Improve

Mix water with dirt and rocks. Slowly pour the dirty water through your filter into a cup. Does the water look cleaner? Does the filter break? Can you make it better? Try again.

Reflect and Share

How big do you think you could make a filter like yours? Could you wash your filter and use it again?

Glossary

cloth

filter

liters

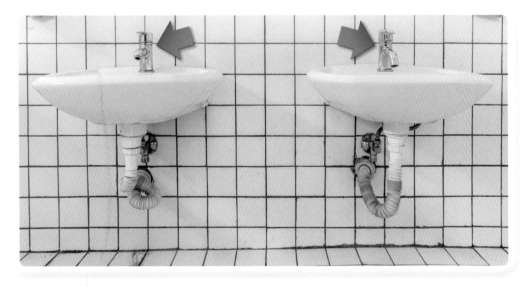

taps

Career Advice
from Smithsonian

Do you want to help all people get clean water? Here are some tips to get you started.

"Fixing big problems means communities and scientists working together. Work to find solutions for everyone." *— Dr. Alison Cawood, Citizen Science Coordinator*

"There are many roles you can play in getting people clean water. Study science, history, and technology. They will give you ideas on how to help people!" *— Dr. Nancy Knowlton, Marine Biologist*